OVERSTOCKED
&
OVERWORKED

How to run an Incredibly successful retail
business and still have a life

STAN KOUROS

Published 2019

Million Dollar Author

Million Dollar Author Publishing
Sydney, Australia

Book Layout © 2019 Million Dollar Author

Overstocked & Overworked. -- 1st ed.
ISBN 9-780994-300768-0-0

Website: www.theretailcoach.com.au

Email: stankouros@theretailcoach.com.au

This book is dedicated to Glynis, Sophie and Zoe for their encouragement and unrelenting support of all my pursuits.

"Retail can be complex or straight forward. Which do you prefer? "

—Stan Kouros

ABOUT THE AUTHOR

Husband, Father, Scientist, Actor, Businessman, AFL tragic, Musician and now...Author.

Stan's career arc has been creative, entrepreneurial and fun. After success as an Actor, Stan co-founded one of Australia's leading Actor Training Institutions and a successful Children's wear Retailing chain. After managing, growing and enjoying the success of these companies for over 30 years he is now focusing his energies on helping wholesale and retail businesses build winning strategies around profit and work life balance.

Stan has always believed in simplifying businesses to a few core principles and helping others find success in life through implementing these same practices.

CONTENTS

CHAPTER ONE

FROM ACTING TO OWNING RETAIL STORES

The day I knew I wanted to be a professional actor was the day I saw my first show at the Princess Theatre in Melbourne. It hit me like a lightning bolt and I had one of those epiphany moments. This is going to be both my creative outlet and my career. I was at High School and immediately signed up for the school musical. They were desperate for boys.

A few years later and after completing a Science degree at Monash University I was accepted into and ended up graduating from NIDA, Australia's National

Institute of Dramatic Art. Life as an actor was wonderful, creative and never boring. I loved it but it didn't lend itself to the great Australian dream and my dream, of a family and a house on a quarter acre block. This was a tough business where only small percentage of actors survive on acting income.

So I was in a business for myself as an actor working away from home again and one day I get a phone call from my wife. Glynis said to me, "Look, you're in Adelaide, you're traveling all over the country to find acting work and we hardly see each other. We need to start a business so we can have a secure income for us and then you can pick and choose the acting work you would like to do and when you're here you can help with the business."

Sounds good, I thought, but what business? What do we know well enough to run as a business?

"Retail!" Glynis said, "Childrenswear retail"

Ok, I come from a family of retailers so maybe we can start a shop and make a go of it, but Childrens wear? So without knowing too much we started a business and fortunately it was a very successful business. We opened our first store in 1986.

I remember the night before we opened that first store we worked until three in the morning ironing and displaying our stock, all the time wondering if anyone was actually going to buy anything from us. Would people like the stock? We had no experience of ranging, pricing, gross profits and final profits. We thought we were filling a gap in the market and we sure hoped the market felt the way we did.

The store was next to an RSL Club and at one stage during that evening an older couple, who I later discovered were regulars at the club, stood outside our front door of the shop and I heard one say to the other, "They'll go broke" My heart sank. Maybe they're right? What are we doing? Fortunately they were very wrong and it was fun giving them a little smile, a friendly smile, every time I saw them waiting for the bus outside our store, as if to say, "We're still here." We were lucky, people did like our stock and the business started growing.

We also knew when we needed help and we found it in a couple of very experienced ex-retailers who were more than happy to give us a hand when we asked. They loved helping because we took their suggestions and acted on them. We did what they said we should to the point where ten years later, we found ourselves having built a home, we had two children, and we were riding the success of our business..... but at what cost?

One day, we realized it wasn't as successful as we thought it was. The failures and the challenges were hidden behind the profits. I mean, we were making good profits, but we were completely stressed out with the running of the business. This was not challenging in a business sense, but challenging in a private sense, because it was difficult for our relationship. We were struggling with balancing everything that needed to be balanced to keep this business going. At that stage, my wife and business partner, who was the Buyer and very important to the success of the business, had resigned about twenty times and I had refused to allow her to resign.

We were so stressed and our kids knew it as well. It was affecting every part of our lives. I thought, "I need to do something. We need to change the way we're doing business or this will be the end of us." We did change and gradually found the answers to running a successful retail business and life outside that business.

So here I am today, thirty six years later, as a sort of, well as a consultant to other businesses, who find themselves in a similar predicament and trying to help them with the answers to find their way out and back to some freedom in their life.

Like many retailers, starting our business, our first store, was really born out of the need to build some consistency to our income, which would enable us to have a family, a roof over our heads and have choice in our life. As much as I loved acting and I was doing okay with that, I loved the idea of a family and providing a great life for them.

What attracted me to a retail business was the familiarity. Retail was in my blood.

I started in retail as a nine year old, with my parents, working behind a counter in a Milk Bar in the 60's wearing a big white coat which all the staff wore in those days. I learned very quickly the principles of good customer service and the basic disciplines like giving the right change and what happened if you gave the wrong change.....your margin and your profit went down. My dad was instrumental in giving me early lessons and disciplines. It didn't seem like much fun when I was going through it at the time but I sure appreciated it later.

Dad's method of training me was to really drop me in the deep end of the pool. I had to sink or swim.
He would show me once how to give change. Fortunately, I was good at mathematics. I do have a science degree, so I can prove that I'm good at math and I enjoyed the math part of it, I enjoyed the money, the coins.

There was an inspiration there to follow that path or become a Doctor or a Lawyer which my parents were hoping for. But then at a certain point in high school I discovered I had a love for creativity and I started to follow that passion more than the passion of what my parents wanted for me.

I completed my science degree at Monash University. Having done that and satisfying my parents need for me to have a degree, I auditioned for NIDA, got in and completed a three year Diploma of Acting.

The love of retail, the understanding of the disciplines of retail, go right back to when I was very young. Like so many migrants my parents set an incredible example of work ethic and focus. They showed me how to really grab an opportunity, grab the strengths you are given and develop your skills, they believed in me. Retail has helped fulfil their aim of creating a new life in a new country with all the security that they had not had in their mother country.

My parents came over to Australia from Greece in the 1950's. My father was from a family of seven children and my mother from a family of five children in a small village in the Peloponnese region of southern Greece. It was after the Second World War when there was not enough food or work to go around and so began the big post war migration to Australia, America and Europe. So many Australians can relate to my story.

So they've got off the boat in Australia, which must have been difficult in a lot of ways but it gave them a lot of opportunities to do things like start up their own little business.

Having parents with a milk bar was pretty cool as a kid. At one stage we lived behind a milk bar which was good and bad. The good things were, there was lots of lollies and milkshakes, although they were rationed, let me tell you. Because that is stock and that affects your final profit if you're eating the stock but my brother and sister and I got our fair share and that was the good thing about living behind our retail shop.

The challenging part was that at that stage, I was about 12 years old and I was absolutely expected to contribute work wise. Mum could hardly speak English but she was learning quickly. We were all learning lots of skills very quickly. So there weren't many parties on the weekend for me or sleep-overs after school. On school days I would come home at about four o'clock. I delayed my homecoming for as long as possible by playing basketball or footy

after school with whoever stuck around. Eventually I had to go home and when I did get home, I was straight on to the shop floor to give dad a break. That's where my roots are, that's for sure.

As people say about those life changing experiences, Retail is in my DNA. I guess it was a form of stability for my parents and a form of stability for me because there's a fairly consistent result that a small business gave in the '60s and '70s. If you were prepared to put in the hours of work and learnt from any mistakes then a milk bar gave you a really good income for a growing family…..and when you think about it, especially when Dad had his family actually running it with him, they weren't paying much for wages. I think we employed one other lady over the two years we were there. So that important measure of wages to sales ratio was pretty good for Mum and Dad.

The milk bar was open every day of the week, including Christmas day afternoon, every day of the year and my parents manned the floor with me. I provided some relief to either of them but they stayed really focused on their plan and they worked really hard to get to their goal. It was very profitable. Those were the days when there was no late night shopping, very few supermarkets and the Shopping Centre complexes were only just getting going. So there was very little competition for night or weekend trade.

The neighbourhood milk bar, or mixed business, was central to the community. There were groceries as well as the bread and milk and cakes and there was a sandwich bar. I learnt about stock control, putting old stock to the front and new stock at the back. I watched and helped Dad write orders as he counted the reserve stock. I helped receive the deliveries of fresh bread and cakes in the mornings before school. That beautiful smell of freshly baked vanilla slices and chocolate eclairs has never left me. There were no computers. Those were the days of the old cash registers and note pads and pens, so you did rely a bit on your math, that's for sure.

I suppose ultimately the biggest lesson I learned was customer service. How to treat people so they're really happy and they'll come back again.

We had many regulars that were doing their weekly shopping with us and their daily shopping too. They were coming back again and again.

There's been a massive change in this whole industry in my lifetime and I've really lived and worked through that massive Innovation and change.

Many of you, reading this are probably thinking, "Yeah, those were the good old days, less competition and more profit."…..and after fifty years working in and around wholesale and retail businesses, what I've discovered is that you can still have those good old days right now, if you keep certain things under control.......

.... And that's why I wanted to write this book.

CHAPTER TWO

THE ROLLER COASTER OF A RETAIL BUSINESS

A roller coaster ride, that's how it felt. Thirty six years of ups and downs in some steep and some more gradual slopes. People long for the good old days of retail because these days the new normal feels more challenging and a lot more complex. Having been on my ride, I realized that the opportunities in this new environment are exponentially greater....if you get a few things right.

The challenges facing retail today are immense. There's the whole new addition of online retailing where just for a start your pricing is easily compared to any other online website. Increasing your margin is not as easy as it used to be by just increasing your prices and providing wonderful service so the customers keep buying.

These days, everything about your business has to be run as close to optimum level as possible. When I started my first store in 1986, as long as you were happy to genuinely smile and treat the customer as a friend, greeting them with a really positive attitude, they would come back. Yes, you did have to have the right stock for your customers but getting hold of the right inventory; the right product offer was and is only part of the challenge. The real challenge is dealing with your forward planning, your margin management and your inventory management in a way that gives you the highest possibility of success.

In our early days there was a little bit of room to move. These days, there's very little, very little margin for error. You've really got to be on your game when you're in retail. But it doesn't have to be as hard as many retailers are experiencing right now and not as hard as it feels when you're in it. There are answers.

When you're hard at it, you feel like there's no certainty. You're not sure if you've got the right or wrong stock, you feel like cash flow is not always there. Sometimes you're selling lots but it's not resulting in money in the bank. You feel completely overwhelmed, like you're drowning in challenges.

There is a way of actually narrowing your focus and once you overcome a small series of challenges everything seems to drop into place. That's because those challenges are the ones that are the most critical and make the most difference and when they are overcome, profits and time seem to open up.

Your time starts to free up, profits increase, and you can make changes to the other aspects of your business you need to improve.

If you get on top of this stuff, you find the personal benefits are significant too…. for one you're sleeping at night. When your business has challenges overwhelming you, you're not sleeping, you're arguing with your partner. You're not happy with your kids. You don't want to spend time with your children, because when you do all you're really thinking about is your business. It's not a way to live life.

For most people who are working in retail, what I've discovered is that if you can really handle a few key challenges in a retail business, it's possible you can have all the things that you dreamed of when you first started including the flexibility to have a life outside of the business. Isn't that why we get into business, so we can be our own boss and live the life we want to live?

For me it gave me the flexibility to pursue acting and pursue other creative endeavors. To also have a business that is flexible, that is profitable and that is fulfilling all the dreams of that childhood business of my parents... providing stability, an income and a secure way to grow.

I know as you are reading this you are realizing that for a lot of retail owners, the reality is almost the opposite. They're stressing about cash in the bank, they're stressing about staffing issues and staring at their stock every day…. "How do I actually deal with this inventory, so that it's working for me?" They're stressing and thinking, "I just don't know what next year is going to look like, or how do I actually compete with all the other retailers and how online retailing can work for us." Far from being the stable bedrock for people to build a life on, it's actually become quite a challenging and uncertain way to earn a living.

When you're on top of your business, when you feel your business is under control, you suddenly find flexibility with your time and you can apportion the right time to be with your family and you are actually with your family. Your mind is there, your body's there, your emotions are there. That's what you were working for when you first started the business.

Well, suddenly when you get the balance right you don't feel like the odd one out, like all you care about is the business and you don't feel like you're missing out as you tell yourself you just have to keep working this hard because that's what being in business is and that's how it's supposed to be. You see your family and the kids relating really well to each other but you're not able to.

My experience tells me when you get to that state where you can let go of your business worries, it gels the family, because your kids can see the difference in you. They know when you're there or your mind's not there. You can't fool them. You might think you can, "Let's go to Luna Park, they can have rides and then I'll be able to just think about the business for a minute.....or make a quick phone call while they're occupied.....check that certain suppliers are doing the things that they need to do or that the staff on the shop floor are managing it the way you would if you were there"

I remember how I would check in and see how the store sales were going at two in the afternoon. "Oh! You're having a bad day... Why are you having a bad day? The weather's really nice. You shouldn't be... Are you approaching every customer? Are you greeting them positively? You are. Okay. Right. Well, just keep doing it, things will change" You try to stay positive but the Staff feel your anxiety and so do you.

Retailing can be such a day to day experience when you're not under control, because you know you're not under control and your fear is it'll get totally out of control and you'll lose everything.

Most of us in retail or wholesale would have had that sense of impending doom. It's such a feeling of failure as a person and a father and a husband and it's scary. It's fearful and it hits you in your stomach.

When you are in that position, you can't see a way out because you don't know what to do. You feel like you're trying everything but you're actually just doing the wrong things. You've sort of drowned yourself in your day to day critical crisis management and you can't see a way through.

I always understood the principles of managing a retail business. After the first successful period of continuous sales growth what I didn't realize was that our expansion had covered up some cracks and the main crack or challenge for us was management of our inventory. We were dealing with a lot of sizes, a lot of SKU's as they say in the business, Stock Keeping Units. We had a range of stock or product offer covering so many different styles and colours over a wide range of sizes. The deception was that our sales were going strong so we thought we were bullet proof but the amount of slow selling stock started to increase and to compensate we opened a new store and another new store, spreading out the stock to make it feel manageable. The problems started to hit home when some of the new stores just didn't work. They were in the wrong location and the product mix was being overshadowed by slow selling stock. We even opened a warehouse to deal with our stock issues.

"Let's get a warehouse. We can get the stock out of the shops and then the shops can be a bit more under control. "It's very easy to suddenly become overstocked. I was standing in my warehouse one day, this was, ten years down the track. I'm standing in our warehouse and the warehouse is totally full of stock. It was a significant size for us. When I say totally full, I mean there was no room for another box. There were clothes hanging on racks. There was stock everywhere. We had a warehouse person and me and then this truck pulled up from a courier and he had thirty-two boxes of stock to deliver! And I just... my heart sank. It was one of those moments where I thought, "Well, I could go into my office and just cry and give up, or I could try and work out a new way of doing this." I'd spoken to enough people, I knew enough about running a retail business. I knew what I had to do but I had sort of procrastinated because it was a whole new project.

At that moment on that day I decided I had to start this new project. It was really Category Management of our inventory, managing our inventory by categorising all our stock. To do that, I had to computerize my stock. Now, I know that sounds ridiculous today, but back then, it was a challenging thing for me. I didn't have five staff in an office with computers everywhere. We had category cash registers, so we could tell what we were selling in terms of amount of tops and bottoms etc. But we had to computerize and use the data so we really understood exactly what we were selling and accurately predict what we needed to order so we could achieve the sales we were aiming for.

What I'm really talking about is; knowing your numbers. Knowing your numbers very, very specifically. My experience is that while we're selling, we feel like we're successful but until we truly know the numbers around what we're selling we are out of control. Once we know what the numbers are in each category, once we understand the margins, once we understand how to manage our stock, so that it's more profitable more frequently, that's the puzzle that I set out to solve.

There was one year, early on, where we actually made really good profits and my accountant said well you've now got this tax bill. I thought, "How am I going to pay for that? And if I've been so profitable, why am I having a problem paying for the tax bill?" So I asked the accountant "Where am I going wrong here?" He said, "Well, you've made a great amount of profit, and most of it is sitting on your racks in the store rooms and in your shops and warehouse." That was a big wake up call. I realized that what was really critical was to know your numbers, so that you're turning that stock into money, at the same time as making profits. You need to know exactly how much stock you need, to make that same profit.

We were terribly over stocked. It had got way out of control and that's the story of a lot of businesses to-day. When you start off in retail, it's very easy to do well in the first two or three years. By the end of about year three, you start having cash flow problems.

There were three key concepts that we discovered in all of this chaos that meant us going from completely out of control to so much more in control. Three key concepts that once understood and put into action made all the difference between having all of the prof-it sitting on our shelves to actually having that profit turn into cash.

CHAPTER THREE

THREE LEVERS FOR TURNING YOUR RETAIL BUSINESS AROUND

The first of the three key levers that made the biggest difference to our business was Forward Planning.

Forward planning made us focus on the coming year's calendar in terms of family, financial, business and social. You thought about daily, weekly and yearly events that were important in those areas and you planned the year ahead. So you had a roadmap of what was going to happen to you, what was in front of you. You worked ahead so you could start to feel on top of your business.

When we worked on forward planning for our business, we were suddenly working on things that weren't expected today or tomorrow and that took the sense of constant crisis out of the business. We looked ahead at dates for the necessities in the running of our stores. The buying seasons, the marketing programs, the staff requirements, financial assessments were all important to finding the rhythm to our business. So you found yourself working ahead of the game and there wasn't the stress of a deadline by three o'clock this afternoon or by Friday of that week. You were talking in terms of months, which was such a change from the crisis management I'd been involved in, in the first 20 years of my business.

And my family could start to count on certain things happening as well and all those events were included in our year's calendar as well.

The second key lever to tackle was Management of our Inventory, or stock.

We understood the concept of Category Management of our stock right from day one, because we had a wonderful consultant who'd spent a big part of his life in retail where he had really focused on category management, so I understood it, but I hadn't really committed to it. At that low point we were talking about earlier, I really knew that I had to commit to what I knew would work and that's managing my stock by managing the categories within it. Anyone in any store or any business, whether it's retail or whole-sale, can divide your stock up into categories and you normally aim for about 10 to 15 categories. You look at the sales history, the purchase history, and the stock levels by category at sell value and you record all that into the right spreadsheet and then you forecast forward in each category. The added difficulty is getting the right spreadsheets giving you the clarity to act and change your results.

The wonder of that is, that with regular monthly reviews of your forecast, and changes according to the changes in business, the flow of the business, you suddenly have clear direction and clear goals by category.

Putting it simply, you're predicting that you're going to sell $1,000 worth of T-shirts next month and you only sell $500 worth. Well, that's okay, because you just adjust what you've put aside to spend on new purchases for t-shirts, so that you're not overbuying. The ideal is to have two to three months' of sales value worth of stock in each category in your store. And if you do that, then you're not going to be over stocked. If you leave yourself room to move, you can adjust accordingly.

This had a profound effect on my state of mind and my relationships with my wife, children and all in the business. Well, I wasn't stressed. I mean, yes, there was a challenge of sales if they weren't going as well as we had predicted, but we knew that ultimately we would be able to handle it financially. It wasn't going to be the ruination of everything we built up, our home. Our security... I didn't have to put everything on the line just to get more stock in so that I could hopefully make a bit more money. I was actually identifying what's working ahead of time and making adjustments for that.

The third key lever is improving your margin, especially your final margin.

If you're not actually making a profit on the item you're selling then you are working really hard for nothing and unless you are really careful with your numbers, you might believe that you are making a profit on that item but you're not. If you don't know what the real profit is, the negative effect ultimately creeps up on you. As I said before, it's very easy to achieve high sales and still be kidding yourself.

One of the worst moments in my business life was that moment where the accountant says, "Wow, you've got a really profitable business. It's a shame that it's all not in your bank, it's actually in your shops."

What do you do? You have a huge sale and you reduce the prices and you try and turn that stock into cash. But of course that affects your final margin.

That balancing act of; when to have a sale, when to reduce items, how much to charge in the first place on top of your true costs, is critical and is made a lot easier by category management. If you've got the right amount of stock in each category, you're not going to be having huge sales when you don't need to. You're not going to be watching your competition for what they're doing, because you know you've got the right stock, in the right items for the customers that are coming through your door or via your website.

Having the right margins, has a huge impact on both the business and the owners state of mind.

We improved our final margin by about 7% once we really got into the swing of category management. Now 7%, if a business is turning over a million dollars, 7% is $70,000. That's a lot of money on your bottom line and in your pocket.

If you're reading this and you're running your own retail business, whatever it may be, fashion, gift, homewares or other you're probably saying, "That's all very good for you. But there are so many reasons why I can't do that." Let's talk a little bit about the three frustrations I hear most from retail business owners.

The most common frustration I hear from retailers when it comes to Forward Planning is….. I'm too busy

What ends up happening is, by not attacking it, by not taking the time to do it, you end up with no certainty. You've got the wrong product offer, you've got staff who are overwhelmed by the amount of stock you've ordered and the stock is in the wrong categories to what is needed….. and your staff are constantly telling you they would have had a better day if only we had more of this or more of that. You're out of rhythm; you're out of step with the key yearly selling seasons or events. That's what happens to you when you fail to plan properly.

You're really busy, you feel overwhelmed and you're going around in circles. You feel like there's just not enough hours in the day to do everything that you need to do. On top of that your staff is saying the results would have been better if only you'd done more. And you're thinking, "Well there's not much more I can do. I'm working day and night on this." But in fact we were working on the wrong things. Once I started working on the right things I stopped being so busy and everything started to change.

When I started to focus on my three Levers or Pillars I still had lots to do, but I was doing it in a totally different spirit. There was a relaxation and a joy in the work and I was working on the future and not the present. I was on top of the business not in the business. I wasn't working on the urgent stuff, instead I was focusing on the important parts of stock, staff & margin. Things that I would normally put off because they weren't urgent, I now found I had the time to complete.

Most people who get into small business have the ability, absolutely. They are also inspired and they're creative and they want to run their own show, because they know it can offer them this freedom.

They're the sort of people who have big ideas. They know the idea they want to get to work on, but they don't allow themselves to get there by the way they approach things day to day.

The second common frustration I discover in retailers is about inventory and stock management. A lot of people running a retail or wholesale business are saying, "Look, I've got plenty of stock and I've got no money, not enough cash flow to cope." When I talk to them about category management I get, "I've got spreadsheets everywhere, what do you mean I've got to do it differently?"

It's really interesting. People who have not experienced good category management methodology just think it's too hard. But if you're already computerized and your stock is already categorized, it's very straight forward to put it into the right software and get the right outcomes. You'll get you there a lot faster and a lot more easily than you thought possible. It just sounds like a whole new thing that you have to do on top of everything else you're doing. But it's the one thing you can do that's going to make your life so much more pleasurable and your business more profitable.

Getting the category management right, really is the linchpin to so many other aspects of your business turning into the kind of business you always wanted to start with.

You really need to think of stock as money. It's your money tied up in your stock. Don't kid yourself that because you like it, it's going to sell at the price that you first put on it. You need data to back you up. You need data to help you make decisions, to understand the customer that's coming through your door. I mean, when we first started business, we used to do this thing which was great. We would record our lost sales. A customer comes through the door and says, "Have you got a white t-shirt in a size four? And you don't have it. The worst thing you can do is just say "Sorry. No, I don't have one" and move on to waiting for the next customer. We would always make a note of the lost sale and our buyer would get a daily report of those lost sales to help her adjust her buying to suit our customers' needs. Just common sense really and it helped enormously.

There are some things that you don't stock, that you just will never carry. It might be a really unusual item that a customer wants that you know doesn't fit into your range. However, if you've recorded that lost sale, you might realize a significant number of people have asked you for that item in the last month and this item now becomes so important and it makes a difference to sales. So we recorded all lost sales and with those lost sales records, we were able to refine our buying. That was the beginning of creating a system that worked for our shops.

To help focus our buying and ease some frustration around inventory buying, or ordering, we learnt the concept of "Good", "Better" and "Best" price points. Three different price points in your best-selling categories. The "Good" price point gives you 20% of your sales in that category. The "Better" price point gives you the majority or 70% of sales in that category and "Best" is just that top 10% of sales which is just window dressing, high priced designer items that give your shop the look and feel that you're after or point of difference, but your best selling price point is in that "Better" range.

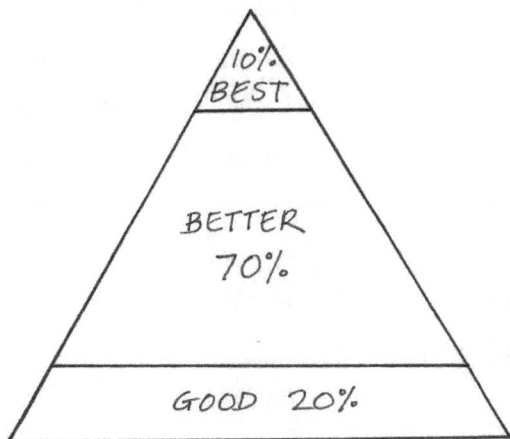

THE PRICE MIX PYRAMID MODEL

"Good, Better, Best"….. Your "Better" selling price point is going to give you your 70% of sales. That's another way of really honing in on what's going to sell for you based on data for what is selling and not some vague feeling while you're in the store or from what your staff feel on any particular day.

All these frustrations and ideas around your stock are cured and tied up with Category Management.

The third major frustration I hear from retailers is around their Margins.

Now the problem for most retailers and the most common objection is, "I can't put my prices up because my customers just won't accept it." That's an objection that we hear across all businesses. There's very few businesses who are telling me, "Hey, I can charge whatever I like." So online retailers have become a major competitor for a bricks and mortar business. Let's look at what's going through the mind of most retailers when we start talking about margins.

Firstly, they might be suffering... They're suffering from no growth in price points. They could be selling a lot of stock and making very little profit. They don't know. The constant price markdowns or sales, leaves them with no way of knowing whether they're actually making or losing money. They could be working really hard for nothing. They've really got to understand what their initial margin is, what their markdowns are, what they've lost from shrinkage, theft et cetera, and what they end up with as their final margin. You've got to be very realistic as to what is the true value of your stock. You might have a shop full of stock that you think is worth what you paid for it and what you're now charging for it, but it might not be and usually isn't because maybe because it has no appeal or is aged or very old stock.

Which is where managing your stock to get the right final margin is critical. The final gross profit margin is the difference in the selling price of your stock to the cost of your stock. Outside of that final margin, on top of that final margin, you've got to take away your expenses. Yes, we do have to control expenses, etc. But what we're talking about here is the retail principles on the shop floor and in your warehouse, to keep that stock moving, get you more stock turns, the number of times you sell your average stock level to achieve your yearly total sales. With the right Category Management System you can work out how much stock you need in each category to achieve the sales for that following month. You will then find you're going to get an increase in stock turns so less money in your stock and more in your bank account.

A stock turn is basically how many times you turn over the total stock in your store in a year. If you sell a million dollars' worth of stock over a full year, and you've got $500,000 at average sell value worth in the store, you've got two stock turns. You need to increase your stock turns by reducing the amount of stock to get the same amount of sales. This will then increase the profitability of your business. Depending on the business you're in, your stock turn needs to be as high as four or five or six, and you can do that by category management, and then you will find your margin will have increased.

In summary, without the three levers in place, what most retail businesses experience and certainly what we experienced as a retailer, was that we were just continually having no certainty about what the week or the month or the year was going to look like sales wise. We felt like we were constantly busy and fairly anxious about checking in on the state of the team, and what was going on in the business. It was so hard to sense what was going on, or any stability, or any hope of a bright future. Any feeling of growth felt very random, like it was in the hands of the gods, whether we grew or not. And it was a very disempowering experience.

If you are experiencing similar problems, and many retailers are, then this is likely where you are at....low or no cash flow to be able to do anything with, to be able to pay for the stock, to pay for the tax bills, to take a family holiday. No certainty, no growth and no cash flow are the frustrations that most retailers will discuss when you get them alone and start talking about life.

But in fact, the opportunity is that the retail business can actually massively increase your earnings. It can give you the kind of stability that it gave my parents when I was young. It can scale your earnings and your money. It's incredible in that it can give you a flexibility of time. It can give you the time back to actually be a father, a husband, an actor, a singer whatever pursuit you want to pursue outside of your business, it has the possibility to give you that flexibility.

For many people it can also give a real alignment to something they feel is meaningful, something creative and something they feel passionate about.

So that while the hope is for more money, more time and more purpose, the reality is that most people are experiencing the exact opposite...no certainty, no growth and very little cash flow.

In the next chapters, we're going to look at the three levers in more depth and specifically the things you can do in order to make immediate changes in your retail business.

1. Forward Planning,
2. Inventory and Category Management
3. Improving your Margin.

CHAPTER FOUR

FORWARD PLANNING

The moment when forward planning really hit home for me, when it impacted me in a big way was actually right at the beginning of my retail journey.

When my wife suggested we start our own business, we looked at the Australian Bureau of Statistics demographics of suburbs that suited our target market. I then took it upon myself to go around and go into similar businesses to the ones we were looking at starting and actually asking if they were for sale? I would go in and say, "Look is this business for sale?" Most would say no, but we'd get talking about the business and they would ask me why I was looking etc? Some people are very happy to share their thoughts with you on the business, so I learnt as I was going. Eventually I found a shop that was for sale, and it actually was in a good position, with good visibility in an area of high disposable income. There were also other existing competitors who had been there for a while so we knew there was a market for Childrenswear. We made an offer and we purchased the business.

What I didn't know, because I hadn't done my forward planning, was that although I'd purchased the business with an existing lease, I still needed approval from the landlord. To get that lease I need the approval of the estate agent and the owner of that building in a suburban strip. I didn't know that. The owners of the business were a local couple. They didn't forewarn me, like me they imagined I would just take over their existing lease as I was buying their business. We set a date for us to settle and for us to take over the store. I proceeded to order all our stock for the store. We had a basic budget. I don't know how we got the budget, but we sort of figured out a budget from what we had and what we were able to borrow.

We had our money saved up and we managed to borrow a little bit more with my father going guarantor to the bank. We then proceeded to order our stock, which then began arriving in our lounge room at home because of course we didn't have a shop. We hadn't moved in yet. One week before we were due to move into the shop, with a lounge room full of cartons of stock, I got a phone call from the owner of the business. (Remember, we were going to settle the purchase at the end of the week.) "Oh, the agent has just said that you haven't been approved as a tenant, you better ring them." Guess what, because we hadn't been in business before the agent was refusing to agree to assign the lease to us.

Wow, that was a bombshell that I didn't see coming…..did not see coming.

We had plenty of stock but no business, no location, no site and most of our life savings and now borrowings in the form of boxes of clothing and toys in our lounge room. What do you do?

You know what I did? I found out who the solicitor was for the owner...I went to their office in the city.....I just turned up. I explained my situation to the receptionist and said that if I didn't see the solicitor I was going to sit in the reception area until he was due to go home and he would have to see me. The solicitor gave in. To cut a long story short, he rang Hong Kong where the owner was and they made clear to me what risks I was undertaking, which were significant, it was a four year lease. I said we're still going ahead, we want to do this. I explained that I'd been in retail since I was nine years old and I knew exactly what I was doing and everything would be fine. Finally, they approved the lease and we got in.

I think my people and acting skills came to the fore. However, I was terrified, of course, because if he'd said no, the stock we had in our lounge room would have been out of date and out of season within a few months. A no would have forced us into looking for another store somewhere. We could have made a rash decision, taken over a store in the wrong position, the wrong area, and it would have been over before we started.

Forward planning is critical. Yes, sometimes you can survive if things go terribly wrong but knowing what's ahead of you, and knowing what's needed in preparation is critical in giving you the best chance of success.

Let's talk about what the critical areas are because forward planning for some people might simply involve thinking about summer, autumn, winter or spring seasons in business but it's more than that.

There are four major areas that we discovered that we needed to focus on with forward planning.

- forward planning your STOCK
- forward planning your STAFF
- forward planning your LOCATION or expansion
- forward planning so you get into the RHYTHM of your business.

Forward planning of stock we know can be to cope with ordering six months ahead if you're in a seasonal fashion business, or day to day ordering if you're in a more immediate, convenience type of business. In either, you still need to be planning ahead. You've got to get an accurate picture of what your particular business requires ahead of time.

With staff, there are different times of the week, month and year where you need more or less staff. That's critical because staff costs are one of your major costs.

With location, there's your other major cost, your rents. Your rents are, again, significant. So the right location in the right area with the right demographic for your product is critical. Plan ahead and allow yourself the time to do the research and give yourself the best chance to make the right choice.

And then the overall rhythm of the business, to do with stock and staff is very important, especially in a seasonal business. But whatever the business, the rhythm of the business is important and needs to be understood.

If you're in the right rhythm with your business, then you feel like you're on top of it. You feel like you're surfing the wave and you're not overwhelmed and swimming against the tide. They're the critical areas where forward planning is essential.

Surfing that wave much like surfing in real life is a thrill and that's kind of what most retailers are looking forward to…being ahead of the game, being innovative and looking to the next thing. It is thrilling, and it's inspiring to get up out of bed in the morning and get into it.

There's nothing worse than waking up and thinking, "I've got to go through all that again today." Waiting for the phone calls, waiting for the next drama to unfold because you haven't thought ahead enough to cover your bases and just minimize those dramas. When you're in the right rhythm you stop thinking in terms of drama. You're thinking in terms of successes and wins and that's what's so inspiring.

Suddenly, it's not hard work. It's just that you're in the flow of your business and your life. So then life isn't hard work either. You move from a state of crisis focus to opportunity focus.....from problems to solutions and then even outside of the business, you move from stressed and absent to actually engaged and present.

Forward Planning and Getting Your Calendar Sorted Out

The first basic area of forward planning is just really getting your calendar sorted. Take the time. Take the time with your partner or your business partner, the important people in your life, to really sort out your calendar in terms of family, social and business.

Plan a year ahead, know what's coming up. What are the important events in that year for you? It's amazing when you put it down on paper, suddenly you feel like you can handle it. It's such a difference to not knowing and just having it just swirling around in your head. Get your calendar sorted. Get your daily, weekly and yearly events down.

Approach planning with this mindset, "What does my ideal week look like? What does my ideal month look like? What does my ideal year look like?" Take the time and rather than think of it as another task on top of all the others, plan your year around, "Okay, I'd like to take a family holiday at this point. I would like to do something for me at this point, or I would like to expand our business at this point". Mapping it out makes it manageable and if it doesn't, you can make rational decisions to change the plan. Looking from that overall perspective gives it a different positive energy.

Urgent, Important, Not Urgent, Not Important

The other thing that I wanted to mention was how we divide up our time between doing what's important and urgent and important and not urgent?

We know the four key areas we're going to try and master in forward planning. You look at each area, stock, staff, location and rhythm. It took me a while but eventually, in the middle of our roller coaster ride, when our business was in real trouble, I finally planned time to think about the important but not urgent things that I would do if I gave myself the space to do them? Those important but not urgent areas are the ones that will make the biggest difference. Find those areas, those projects and plan to make a start and plan to complete them.

Forward Planning Stock

With stock the important but not urgent project I kept putting off was computerizing and looking at systems that would give me the right data. You'd want to make sure that if you need to change your system, that you're working on that. You're thinking ahead on that. Ahead of what's happening day to day with your stock. You're looking at improving your system. You're not going to be satisfied with the one you've got today if it's not doing absolutely everything you need it to do and giving you every bit of information you need. And it's so much easier than you think.

This is critical to the success of Category Management, which we'll go through later.

Forward Planning Staff

With staff you're not looking at the day to day basics which are important and urgent like how they're treating customers, but you're actually starting to think about, "Maybe I need to look at the culture in my business around staff, and what I can do to improve the staff engagement or ownership in my business?"
The bigger picture, the bigger idea of culture, not just the basics of "This is what you do at the counter, how you fold the clothes, this is how you put things on display etc. All the basics are important but we're not just talking about the basics.

When we plan ahead we make time to start talking about what it takes to help your staff be positive at work so you feel happy that they are really invested in their job, they are really enjoying their work. "How do I get my staff to take ownership of the business and treat it like it's their business?"….It can happen by thinking and planning forward, not present but into the future.

Forward Planning Location

Consider your location and think into the future. Where am I now? The business or businesses I've got now, are they going to survive in the locations we're in? The leases I have...

Let's look ahead, let's spend time building the relationships with my landlords. Let's be looking into what's happening in retail generally and seeing if it might be worth a move or not..... before you sign the next lease. Spend the time to get all the facts and check with your accountant, solicitor and those close to you, whose advice you trust.

Forward Planning is really about getting out of the urgent demands of your day to day stuff and stepping out to look at the important bigger picture. To make this happen you need to start thinking, "Should I be doing this task?" "Is there anyone in my business who could be doing this task now, so I could be looking at those other bigger picture items?" You'd be amazed how much of the day to day stuff you can just delegate to staff keen to step up and take some ownership.

In our business, forward planning meant we ended up selling the business profitably so not just for the value of our stock but for the goodwill of our business name... our brand. I knew I had to have an exit strategy. Eventually, you have to give yourself the most profitable way out. That was done by implementing some really great stock management, category management. Getting my big ideas in place, and then being able to, at the right time, have a profitable business to sell." And a profitable business will sell, and we were able to do that.

That's certainly the dream of most people who start a retail business. You dream of building something valuable and then find someone to pass that on to and draw some the value out of that sale so that you can move on to the next project.

And my next project is this......to help people get through their journey and find their freedom in retail.

In summary, without forward planning you have no certainty. You can have the wrong stock, disinterested staff, difficult location and you're out of rhythm or step with the key yearly events of your business and your life.

With forward planning;

You have the right stock for the season at that time.

Your staff are much happier and positive and are taking ownership and helping you build the right culture for your business.

You make the right choices on location with the basics in place like customer parking and visibility to large groups of people.

And you are in step with the key yearly changes for your business and your life......

You're on your way to freedom.

CHAPTER FIVE

STOCK MANAGEMENT

Let's talk a little bit about the second lever, Inventory or Stock Management. This is a big one. This is probably the area where most people can make an immediate improvement in their business.

We can look at the four key areas of Stock Management;

- Sales and the 80/20 rule.
- What Data we need to be looking at.
- Stock Cycles particular to our business.

- And finally identifying the Market Trends.

The first year or two in our business was really exciting and it is for most of us because you're making sales, you're new, hopefully new customers are discovering you every day and it feels like it's just going to go forever, this growth is going to go forever. What happened to us was, after about two years full of confidence and optimism for the future, our buying got out of control, mostly because we just believed we could sell anything. Any amount of stock that we bought, we thought we were going to sell because we thought we were so good at it. Then it hit us. Came the end of the season, all the stock had arrived and we still had a shop full of stock and the season was about to change over.

The winter stock that we bought, so confident that we were going to sell and improve our sales dramatically again, hadn't all sold. We'd made some mistakes which everyone does. We knew we had to change certain things then and we did. We knew very quickly that it wasn't as simple as just buy everything and everything will sell.

It really hit our cash flow. One minute you're antici-pating, "Okay, we're going to have some money in the bank and we can do things with that." And then the next minute, everything dries up. We had no stock management system in place that allowed us to budg-et and plan for our buying.

We were basically left with a lot of styles that were either not selling at the prices we had put on them, our normal mark-up, or we just had too much quantity in those styles. We'd run out of a few best sellers and we weren't able to repeat on them because we had no money to buy more. Very quickly, it was going to be the wrong stock for the wrong season.

We had a mountain of numbers and data that was to-tally confusing and meaningless. We had to very quickly simplify the data. As well as being very lucky with a really great end of season sale. Taking advice from a very experienced retailer, we were able to turn most of that stock into cash and we were on our way determined that we didn't make the same buying mis-takes again.

We managed to get over that hurdle very quickly because we took the advice and acted on it straight away. We found out that the mistake a lot of people make is they don't cut their losses. They don't accept that they've made mistakes and take immediate action. .....because there's an anticipation of, "I want that stock to be worth this much money," and the reality sometimes really slaps you in the face.

You've got to accept reality. Retail can be brutal and you don't want it to destroy you.

If you don't accept reality, then what that leaves you with in a lot of ways is a desperate action. You get in a dire situation and you've got to hold a massive sale and in our case that was successful but some of the Hail Mary passes that people have to do in retail don't always work out that way.

One of the mistakes we all make is, "Let's have a sale, but my stock is so good I'll just reduce it by 20% and everyone will love it and buy it at that price." And then it doesn't sell at 20% off, so we go, "Well, let's go to 30% off." By the time we've got to 40% off, and still sitting with a shop full of stock, it's too late.

Your first markdown is your best mark down.

We very quickly learned that principle. If you've made a mistake, you need to quit your slow movers as quickly as you realize. You take a bigger mark down and you get it out of your store, you turn that stock into money quickly and you can then invest that money in stock that is selling. This applies to all businesses selling stock or merchandise. If it hasn't moved in say six weeks then mark it down and get rid of it.

The 80/20- Rule and Knowing Your Data

The 80/20 rule, what 20% of our stock is providing 80% of our sales and what is my data system telling me?

That's a question you should be asking yourself month in month out.

At the beginning of every month, you review the previous month and you get your numbers and you adjust your "available to spend". Or, how much spare money do I have in my adjusted budget to spend in each category, for the coming month, to give me the best chance of reaching my targeted sales.....what 20% of each category is driving those sales? So really knowing your data and your numbers; which is the second critical element of inventory and stock management.

Getting your systems right to give you the data you need and applying the right principles with that data is an area that we'll look at in more detail later in the book.

Stock Cycles and Market Trends.

You've got to understand the stock cycle of your business, so that you can be working ahead of the cycle and certainly not behind what your customers expect. Because no matter what season you think it is, it's what the customer is trained to think that you need

to understand. This is especially important in fashion. But fashion is not just in clothing and accessories. Fashion is relevant to a lot of different categories. Homewares is another fashion influenced category of merchandise. You've got to be up with the latest trends. Ordering to those cycles, those market trends is critical for giving your stock the best opportunity to sell and telling your customers that your shop should be their first stop for your category of merchandise.

There's buying and there's selling and they're equally as important because if you're not buying the right stock, the right amount of the right stock, then you're not going to be selling as much as you want to.

Buying the right stock is, knowing your stock cycles and knowing what the market trends are, so you can predict and order the right product mix or product offer for your customers' needs. Market trends, stock cycles, having the data to give you the information, having that data, the numbers, is critical. And then with selling, knowing that you're never going to run out of your 20% of stock that's giving you the 80% of your sales will boost your sales rapidly.

When we talk about stock cycles, we're talking about how effectively you are buying and how often you sell out all of the seasonal or cyclical stock in your store. On a simple level, that's it.

That certainly describes a stock cycle in fashion retailing. It's winter and summer with a little bit of autumn and spring thrown in. But we're effectively talking winter fashion and summer fashion cycles. In other businesses, the cycles will be different. The cycles and trends might be governed by whether we're talking battery operated or petrol powered tools. What are the hot items at the moment? With healthcare and pharmacies, the cycles include flu season and travel season. Whatever your business is, it has a stock cycle and you need to be on top of it and plan ahead for it.

Certainly Christmas is critical for most businesses. That's a critical part of your cycle, that you need to be planning for months and months ahead to get the most out of.

When I started, I certainly had a simplified idea of seasonal stock cycles. I thought Summer was Summer ie December, January, February. Little was I to know that the stock cycle in my business was that Summer was from the middle of July through to Christmas and that's your long seasonal cycle. You might be in real trouble if you've got too much stock after Christmas because yes, there is a Summer, but generally, your Winter stock starts arriving in the middle of January. Your Winter seasonal cycle is from the middle of January right through to the end of June when the Summer stock starts arriving. The seasonal cycle is very different to what you as a person might imagine before you get into that business. And again that's where your forward planning is important. Knowing what you're getting into ahead of time.

The impact of successful stock management is really profound for most people. Rather than experience no cash flow, when you get the inventory and the stock right, you can suddenly be flush with cash. You realise you've got money in the bank and the stock has turned into cash, and you now have opportunity. You can reinvest that in growing your business and grow-

ing your family assets. You can use that to buy property, to have a well-earned holiday. It really switches everything. The business starts to pay off like it did for us.

And, it gets you racing, it's exciting. Because suddenly, you feel like you've unlocked the door to prosperity and it feels so simple. It feels so easy. When you've really understood your inventory, and you're really on top of it with numbers and you're ahead of the cycle and you know your market trends and you're buying the right product to give you the best return. You just feel like you could have flexibility, certainty and real purpose back in your life.

You're sleeping better, you've got a more positive relationship with your partner and your children. You're waking up in the morning excited about the day ahead and you're giving yourself time to be creative with the future in terms of your personal life and your business life and it's a joy.

It's a joy and it's a great way to live.

Unfortunately, a lot of retail business owners are finding themselves waking up at two o'clock in the morning stressed about all the urgent crises that might happen, before they've happened, in the day coming up.

Effectively with inventory and stock, category management is a straightforward simplification of your inventory, which allows you to improve your rotation of stock by identifying slow movers and bestselling categories. It gives you a clear buying plan that takes the guesswork out of stock management, and ultimately cash flow. There's no guesswork. You can use the experience that you've gained in your business with the data that you're receiving, to make really good clear decisions and there's no guesswork.

That's the result we should all be looking for, I think.... that gives you the freedom in your life.

So even though what you're doing is managing stock, what you're actually doing is developing freedom and joy in your life and your work.

CHAPTER SIX

MARGINS

The third important lever of running this retail business that's both profitable and gives you your life back is dealing with your margins.

I think the story that comes to mind is a very real experience, about running a business that you believe is running successfully, in that you're selling things and you're achieving growth in your sales but ultimately, you're not making money. You're not making profits that you think you deserve to be making, given the amount of sales you're achieving.

If you don't get margins right, what you're doing is you're working really hard, you're making a lot of sales, you appear successful but the money in the bank that you get to take home at the end of the day just isn't there. So you're doing a lot of work for not much progress.

I think what's currently happening in retail is you get customers who are into this SALE mentality. Without really wanting to, the department stores and a lot of the big brands have now trained their customers to not buy unless something is reduced. If you're in that cycle, you're really harming your margin. In our business, we decided not to compete on regular price reduction SALES but focus on, having the right stock when our competitors were out of stock and great customer service. So there's a way of not being in that cycle, which is having the right stock for the customer when they come in at the right time of year.

Primarily what's happening is, customers have a choice between online stores, Department stores and High Street shops or Independent retailers. Every retailer today has to have a website alongside social media to survive, that's a given. But why can't you be competitive by having the right stock rather than always having to reduce the price of your stock?

Managing your stock to be buying specifically what you need is the answer and having that there when that customer goes onto your website or into your store. If you're buying it correctly, if you're buying it at the right price, you can still have specials etc. and monthly promotions to entice your customers.... but you're still making the right final margin because you've bought correctly.

So, the four key areas of margins to focus on are;
- Your true cost, understanding what each item in your inventory truly does cost you.
- Your margin management, which we just spoke about.
- Your pricing, get the pricing structures right.
- Managing your markdowns or price changes.

Let's look at the essential things to keep in mind for these four areas of Margins.

Knowing the True Cost

The cost of an item is the price that the supplier puts on that item. The true cost takes into account any discounts or rebates that you have received from your supplier of the item. Discounts and rebates can be for large or volume purchases or for paying your supplier quickly, or even to help you sell the item at a reduced price. These discounts can have a big effect on your final profit.

Margin Management

Margin management needs to take into account the cost of running your business, the cost of doing business. You need to set your selling prices so that you cover your expenses and make a healthy profit while competing with other related retailers. You also need to take into account loss of stock through theft and damage which can dramatically affect your chances of success or otherwise.

The best way we found when buying our stock, was to work from the selling price that you think you can get for an item, back to the cost price you're prepared to pay to give you your required margin. That is why we always managed our stock by the selling value and not by the cost value. It was the only way to accurately see what was happening to our final achieved margin.

Pricing

On top of managing your margins you need to get your systems around pricing to be as accurate as possible. Human error can have a big effect on your profits as well. To lessen the errors get the systems and structures around pricing simplified and more certain.

Managing Markdowns

When you record and analyze your data at the selling price or sell value, you are able to clearly see the effect of markdowns on your profit margins. You have a chance to manage your markdowns. As I said before, the sale mentality of retailers today makes it so important that they have a way of consistently seeing what is happening to their margin. You need to know monthly but so many are struggling to accurately record what's happening, until that day at the end of the financial year when the accountant gives them the bad news. Markdowns are such a critical factor in your retail outcomes and you need to have a system of managing them. Thank goodness we found ours. It's a very affordable software package program called MFP, Merchandise Financial Planning and I became proficient at using the program for the management of the three retail levers that made the difference to our business outcomes. I've got a section of my book coming up that shows you the way MFP can change your outcomes too.

For now let's continue focusing on Margins and sum up. In pricing, as we've mentioned before, the concept of the 'Good' 'Better' 'Best' price points is an important structure to your buying. In your best-selling categories give people a choice of price points. Again, Markdown management is really important. Reducing your markdowns so that your final margin is improved. Markdowns can destroy a business. Yes, you can achieve more sales but it's at the cost of final margin, which ultimately doesn't cover your expenses and you're working for nothing which is completely crushing.

If you're not up to date with your data and your numbers, the 'dark times' as experienced by me and by most retailers, at these critical stages where you're so drowned under your day to day work that you really don't understand where your business is at, one day it all hits you. Your accountant says,

"Look, you had great sales, but I'm sorry to say you actually haven't made much profit."

That is a soul destroying discussion to have. You really feel like giving up. But actually you know you can't, you're stuck. It's your pride; your reason for working so hard suddenly takes the biggest hit. Embarrassing is just too light a word. Successful work life is part of your identity. You feel crushed. You've put so much energy and time into this and you have made sacrifices. You feel like it's been a total waste of time and you've led your partner and your family astray. And you've worked bloody hard doing it...... that's how I felt at the bottom.

When you get that wrong, when you get the margin wrong, it not only has an effect on the business but it powerfully affects you as the owner, both personally, emotionally and work-wise as well.

But with the right help I found the opportunity is actually pretty bright. Most people are worried about online businesses and how they're affecting their margins but actually the opportunity is really bright in terms of margins.

It all comes back to buying the right stock for your customers' needs. That understanding can save a business.....buying the right amount of the right stock for the right time of year. If you know your true costs, you manage your pricing, your margins and your markdowns to a plan, then you've got certainty around profit and you're not waiting with this dread of, "Am I working really hard and making nothing? I don't real-

ly want to know. I'll just keep working hard and hopefully it'll work out." You need to give yourself more
certainty.

"Sooner or later, if I just work hard enough something
good is bound to happen", is a mantra that a lot of
people in retail live by. But it's not the best way and
that's what I'm trying to help retailers see. There are
ways of finding freedom in a retail business and
they're not that hard. How much better would it be to
be living knowing you can say to yourself......

"I know my true costs and have managed my pricing,
margins and markdowns to a plan that gives me real
certainty around the profits of my business?"

Improving margins is the third step to freedom in
your life.

CHAPTER SEVEN

MINDSET MODELS & PRACTICAL HELP

1 – Planning For Success

SWIMMING
RETAIL PRINCIPLES
AHEAD OF CYCLES
MAX PROFIT

NO PLAN
REACTIVE
LOW MARGINS
DROWNING

THE PLAN FOR SUCCESS MODEL

I have a model that I call 'Plan for Success'. This is just a simple diagram which gives you the upside and the downside of your actions. It's a reminder for your mind, your thought process. On the upside you've got to have your retail principles in place and you've got to be ahead of your cycles to maximize profits and I call that swimming, you're swimming. On the downside if you've got no plan, you're reactive to the competition and you've got low margin sales, then you're drowning. It's a clear example of what you really need to focus on.

2-The Freedom Circle

I have the Freedom Circle, which is just a graphic reminder of the three key principles, the three key levers that we've discussed; Inventory, Planning, and Margins. If you can get on top of those three key levers then you're going to find freedom. So that's the freedom circle.

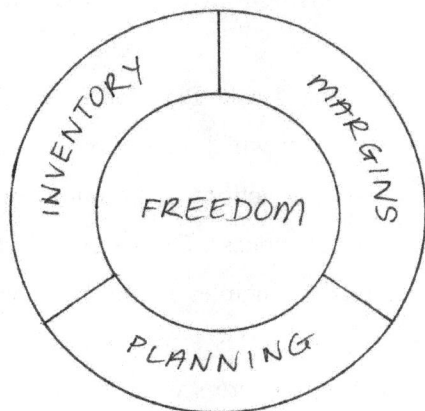

THE FREEDOM CIRCLE MODEL

3- The Prosperity Matrix

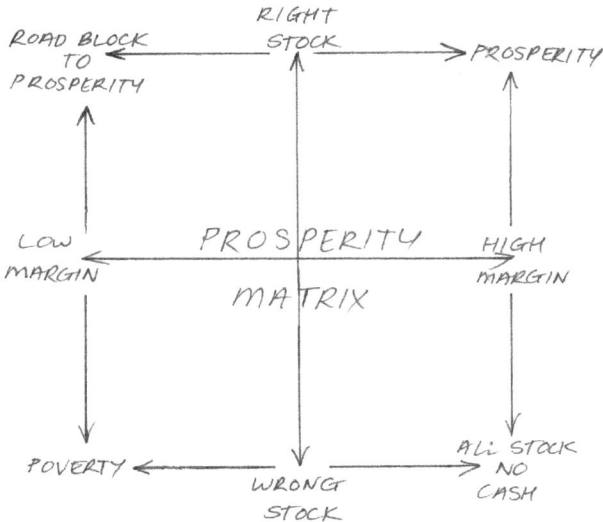

THE PROSPERITY MATRIX MODEL

I have the prosperity matrix, which is a really clear example of what happens when you have the right stock at a high margin and not the wrong stock at a low margin. What you're aiming for is the right stock at high margin sales, giving you prosperity. The wrong stock at low margin sales are going to give you poverty. The right stock at a low margin, well that's a roadblock to prosperity. That's a big roadblock. All stock and no cash is what you get with high margin and the wrong stock. That's my prosperity matrix.

4- Five Steps to Category Management

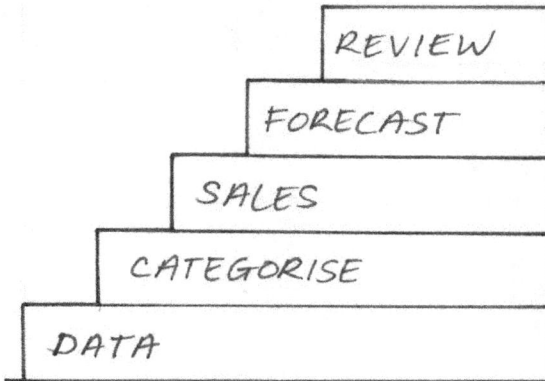

THE FIVE STEPS TO CATEGORY MANAGEMENT MODEL

And really, to sum up what I truly feel about the success pathway in retail, I've come up with the five steps to category management. Your first step is get your data right. Get your system, your data right. The next is categorizing your stock into the main categories in your business. Every item has a category. Then get your sales history data sorted, so you know what you've sold in every category and what you bought in every category and what you've actually got in stock in every category. Then using the Merchandise Financial Planning MFP program you can forecast ahead, you can forecast a buying plan for each category that will give you certainty around sales. Review that forecast monthly. Stay on top of it and adjust as you go. It's fluid, it's flexible. It's a great way cf managing a retail business. I'm saying climb the ladder to category management. Get on board.

CHAPTER EIGHT

GETTING SOME HELP

So, the reason I'm doing this work is to show retail businesses how to become more profitable and help their owners find freedom. By focusing on Forward Planning, Inventory and Margin, a business can significantly improve its cash flow, certainty and opportunity for growth giving the owners more time, flexibility, money and purpose in their lives.

If you're reading this book and you want to know how to get more help, here are a number of ways you can connect.

Don't hesitate to email me. We can set up a meeting and I can take you through the principles of category management and the MFP program. This is a purpose built program which is designed to be easy to follow and very quickly gives you a true and clearer picture of where your business is at. With that picture you can then go forward in your retail business with some certainty. That's a piece of software that is available to any of my clients.

Now, there's a number of ways of connecting with us. If you're in retail and you're thinking, "You know what, it really is hard to see the wood for the trees and I would really like someone with the experience and the tools to help me have some outside perspective on our business."… Then what you really should do is to book yourself in for one of our 15 minute 'Triage' sessions. What we aim to do in the session is find out where you're at now, where you'd like to be and what the roadblocks are. That's a FREE session. We do that session free because we know that out of all the people that actually do that session, there's going to be a few people that actually want some further help and we're here to give that help.

After your free session, if it's not for you, that's ok. You'll go away with a clear idea of what to work on to turn your retail business around.

For those who want some extra help, we've got one to one coaching. We have a program where we come in and work with you specifically on your retail business to move you to the next level. But what we also have is our exclusive members program. This is where we create a community of people who are all working on this more specific targeted program and we go through all the contents of this book in more depth, month by month improving your retail business as we go. The great thing about that is that not only are you getting the content, you're getting a community of people who are supportive and are sharing similar experiences in business.

If there's one thing to know for every one of you who are reading this book, is that running a retail business can be a very lonely experience. So we want to be able to surround you with support. We want to surround you with a community that wants us all to win.

Also, there are one day workshops and short six week programs. Wherever you are on the scale of needing assistance, we've got a way to help that will suit you. Contact us by the email first and then we'll have a website for you to go and check out further.

Website: www.theretailcoach.com.au
Email: stankouros@theretailcoach.com.au

Find us on Facebook. Overstocked and Overworked

www.ingramcontent.com/pod-product-compliance
Lightning Source LLC
Chambersburg PA
CBHW030532210326
41597CB00014B/1121